An Easter Walk

From Palm Sunday to the Ascension
Forty Devotions

Zan Marie Steadham

Barbara,
I hope you always know the joy and peace of God's love.
Thea

✝✝✝   *Steadham*

*An Easter Walk
From Palm Sunday to the Ascension*

Copyright © 2009 Zan Marie Steadham
ISBN 978-0-615-32638-2

First Printing 2009
By API Print Productions

All rights reserved. No part of this book may be reproduced, utilized in any form, or stored in any retrieval system without permission in writing from the author.

All scripture quoted is from the *Holy Bible, New International Version*, published by B. B. Kirkbride Bible Co., INC. and Zondervan Bible Publishers, 1983. Used by permission of Zondervan Publishing House. All rights reserved.

Cover design by Zan Marie Steadham.
Cover photo courtesy of Microsoft Clip Art—www.microsoft.com/en-us/clipart/default.aspx

An Easter Walk ✞✞✞

Introduction

Easter was a colorful time when I was a child. From the color of the crinkly artificial grass we chose for our ribbon-bedecked Easter baskets to the rainbow hues of our boiled eggs. The ritual of dyeing eggs was one my sister, brother, and I looked forward to from Palm Sunday to the Saturday before Easter. From the basic red, yellow, blue, and green food colorings, we concocted lovely turquoise, sunset red-orange and beautiful chartreuse. Mother even allowed us to dip the last few in all the colors to produce a startling shade of muddy gray.

If we thought beyond dyeing eggs, we wondered how much chocolate would show up in our baskets on Easter morning. None of us really stopped to think about the purpose of Easter beyond studying our Sunday School lesson. Christmas was a different matter. Even now we spend much more time thinking and preparing for Christmas than for Easter. Some people start shopping during the after-Christmas sales. Others wait until Christmas Eve. Either way, you cannot ignore our culture's emphasis on preparing for Christmas.

✝✝✝ Steadham

What about Easter? After all, Easter *is* the reason there is a Christmas. Preparing for Easter is the focus of the Season of Lent. Many see it as a time of repentance for sins committed during the year and reflection on Christ's sacrifice. *An Easter Walk from Palm Sunday to the Ascension* was written to contemplate Christ's purpose and mission and to consider the importance of following Christ's steps throughout the year. Whether we are on the road to Emmaus as a believer who doesn't fully understand and believe everything Jesus has said, or on the road to Damascus as an adamant unbeliever, or somewhere in between, we can all experience the Living Lord during our Easter walk and for the rest of our lives.

Many churches recognize this season though they celebrate it differently. Whatever our tradition is, it is vitally important that we prepare our hearts and minds to worship Christ each Easter. Dr. Steve Davis challenged our church to do this type of preparation during the 2005 Season of Lent. My personal response to this challenge was studying the events of Holy Week. As I read the scripture depicting each event, I realized that I had to respond to what I was reading and began to write my responses down. I hope my reactions to the story of Christ's Easter walk will lead you to prepare to worship Christ more fully and deeply.

An Easter Walk follows Christ step-by-step on His last trip to Jerusalem and the Temple; to His last sermon and last prayers; and His glorious victory over sin, death, and separation from God. Following His Easter walk shows why He alone is worthy of our praise, why

An Easter Walk ✝✝✝

He alone is the Savior. The events are presented in a logical day-by-day sequence.

The devotions begin with a verse from the scripture recounting that event. At the end, the reader is invited to a fuller walk using the full scripture references that were used to prepare each devotion. The forty devotions can be used one a day during Lent, starting on Ash Wednesday as is practiced in many Catholic and Protestant churches or on Clean Monday (the Monday after Ash Wednesday) as is practiced in many Orthodox churches. Please note that in the tradition of Lent starting with Ash Wednesday, the forty days do not count the six Sundays between Ash Wednesday and Easter. Traditionally, these Sundays are focused on topics concerning the Resurrection in honor of Easter. I have included a poem for each of these Sundays and for Easter Sunday. The devotions may be read any time the reader wants to appreciate the sacrifice Our Lord made for us.

May *An Easter Walk* help us all to prepare our hearts, minds, and souls to be a temple for the Holy Spirit. May it help us to prepare our lives so we may be receptive to Christ's love. May we clean out the distractions of things, jobs, fears, and worries to be usable in Christ's will. May *An Easter Walk* help us all to experience the Living Lord in our lives.

☙❧

Ad Gloriam Dei
To the Glory of God

An Easter Walk ✞✞✞

Day 1
Triumphal Entry

"Blessed is the king who comes in the name of the Lord!"
"Peace in heaven and glory in the highest!" Luke 19:38

Who was this man riding into Jerusalem this morning? Why were the crowds so enthusiastic? Many knew He had raised Lazarus from the dead. They were curious. Amazed by such power, they shouted, "Hosanna! Blessed is He who comes in the name of the Lord!" Luke's account adds, "Peace in Heaven and glory in the highest!"

Did they really want peace or did they want a conqueror to throw hated Rome out of their country? He answered them by riding on a donkey, not a horse, because the kings of Israel rode horses during war and donkeys during peace. He had repeatedly said, "My kingdom is not of this world."

✟✟✟ *Steadham*

What solutions are you seeking for the turmoil in your life—work, bills, illness, family? Would a peaceful resolution to all the conflicts be one of your desires? There is only one source of peace. During our Easter walk, may we all turn to Jesus, the Prince of Peace for He is the one source of true peace. May we all join in and say, "Hosanna! Blessed is He who comes in the name of the Lord!"

For a further walk, see
Matthew 21:1-11
Mark 11:1-11
Luke 19:29-44
John 12:12-19

An Easter Walk

Day 2
Cleaning the Temple

"It is written," He said to them, "'My house will be a house of prayer'; but you have made it 'a den of robbers.'" Luke 19:46

Don't you know you yourselves are God's temple and that God's Spirit lives in you? 1 Corinthians 3:16

Can a sacred place be defiled? According to Christ, the answer is yes. As He entered the Temple in Jerusalem His last Passover Week, He found merchants changing money for the many pilgrims and selling doves for the sacrifices. Noise, argument, and greed were defiling the sacred place. Jesus cleansed the Temple for true worship and the dwelling of the Most High God. With a righteous anger that surely startled even those who had traveled with Him for three years, Jesus overturned the tables and scattered the moneychangers. The high priests had profited greatly from this defilement and now Jesus had called them to account.

✝✝✝   *Steadham*

Holy Week is a good time to assess ourselves as the dwelling place or the temple of the Holy Spirit. What do we need to clean out of our lives, hearts, souls, and minds to be a fitting temple? What do we need to overturn to be receptive to God's love? Clean out the distractions of things, money, jobs, fear, worries, and stress. During our Easter walk, may Christ make us usable for His Holy will!

For a further walk, see
Matthew 21:12-13
Mark 11:15-17
Luke 19:45-46

Related Passages
1 Corinthians 3:16
2 Corinthians 6:16

An Easter Walk

Day 3
By What Authority?

Jesus entered the temple courts, and, while He was teaching, the chief priests and the elders of the people came to Him. "By what authority are You doing these things?" they asked. "And who gave You this authority?" Matthew 21:23

The chief priests and elders of the Temple were on a mission Holy Week. They sought to discredit the upstart Galilean teacher whom the people adored. Jesus' triumphal entry on Palm Sunday had horrified and energized them. So, a group came to Him in the Temple and asked one of the central questions concerning Him—"By what authority do you teach?"

Jesus answered with a question—"By what authority did John baptize—Heaven or Hell?" As with many of His questions, Jesus pointed to the heart of the matter. They saw the problem and knew either answer would hurt their status. If they answered by Heaven, they had to explain why they were not among John's followers. If they answered by Hell, they would anger John's large numbers of followers. Their cowardly answer was, "We don't know."

Jesus proceeded to show their attitude through two parables. In the story of the two sons, He showed the wickedness of hypocrisy and reminded the leaders of their claim to follow God while condemning other sinners. In the second story, He showed the murderous greed of the tenants who killed the heir and reminded the leaders of their insistence that Jesus could not be the Son of God.

On our Easter walk, may we return to the original question—by what authority did Jesus speak, live, die, and save? We all must answer for ourselves this central question. Our answer will show by what authority we live our lives and our lives will show our answer.

For a further walk, see
Matthew 21:23-41
Mark 11:27-33, 12:1-9
Luke 20:1-16

An Easter Walk ✝✝✝

Day 4
Questioning Jesus

Later they sent some of the Pharisees and Herodians to Jesus to catch Him in His words. Mark 12:13

As Holy Week continued and more people joined the crowd around Jesus, the leaders (Herodians, Pharisees, and Sadducees) tried to trap Him with tricky questions. Their agenda was simple. They wanted to discredit Him with the crowd and end the idea that Jesus could be the Messiah. They came with their assumptions that He could be tricked either into admitting that He was not God or into provoking the Romans into arresting Him.

The Pharisees and Herodians posed the first question. Should we pay taxes to Caesar? The Pharisees would gain power if the answer was no and the Herodians would gain if the answer was yes. Each sought to use Jesus to strengthen their position among the people. Jesus asked for a coin and showed that Caesar made it so giving it back would be reasonable but He also added that what God gave should be returned to God. This confounded both groups.

Next, the Sadducees tried. Their assumption that there were no resurrections prompted a question about how to interpret and apply a little-used Levitical law—which of seven successive brothers would be married to the same wife in Heaven. Again, Jesus referred them to the source—God. Since God declared Himself to be God to the Patriarchs long after their physical death, they were alive and resurrected. His questioners were again dismayed and frustrated in their attempt to trip Him.

The third was a question from a scribe. He didn't come with the usual assumptions and asked what was the Greatest Commandment? When Jesus summarized the first four commandments in loving God and the last six in loving others, the scribe agreed. Jesus commended him for understanding that these attitudes were far more important than burnt offerings and sacrifices.

During our Easter walk, what do we want to ask Jesus? We must lay all our assumptions about His answers at His Cross. Ask, and it will be answered.

For a further walk, see
Matthew 22:15-40
Mark 12:13-34
Luke 20:20-40

An Easter Walk ✝✝✝

During His Easter Walk

He found
    No kingdom of men,
        But one of Heaven.
    No gold for a crown,
        But one of thorns.
    No bone was broken,
        Only His heart.

He gave His life in sacrifice
To save our lives and souls.

೩೦೦೩

Day 5
The Widow's Mite

Calling His disciples to Him, Jesus said, "I tell you the truth, this poor widow has put more into the treasury than all the others. They all gave out of their wealth; but she, out of her poverty, put in everything—all she had to live on." Mark 12:43-44

Have you ever found yourself looking at how little you have and saying, "Surely, God can't use this! It's too small! My time, talents, and money are just not enough to support the Kingdom of Heaven."

Or, have you in your abundance calculated the tithe to the last penny and smugly said, "Here's Yours, God. I'll enjoy the rest I have worked so hard for. Surely, my money is all You need to support the Kingdom of Heaven and Your will."

Remember what Jesus said about the poor widow who gave her offering out of her poverty. She gave more than the rich did. In fact, she had given her entire living. It wasn't the larger amount, but it was her spirit overflowing with gratitude for God's care and faith that

An Easter Walk ✞✞✞

He would keep providing. Her offering to give all she had proves her commitment.

During our Easter walk, we should strive to honor Jesus' offering of His life by seeking to freely give of all He has given us. May we be as generous as the widow, for all we possess is a gift of an infinitely generous Lord and Savior.

For a further walk, see
Mark 12:41-44
Luke 21:1-4

Day 6
The Seed

I tell you the truth, unless a kernel of wheat falls to the ground and dies, it remains only a single seed. But if it dies, it produces many seeds. John 12:24

What is a seed? Do you look at one and see only the seed, or do you see a plant ripening and bearing many more seeds? Jesus saw the latter, but He also saw the truth—the potential harvest cannot be reached unless the seed dies and is buried. Is this harsh? Some of us think so. We want to serve Jesus, but we want to keep our comfort and possessions. We don't want to die to our old lives in order to bear witness to Jesus.

Jesus also knew that He had to die to produce seeds. He told the crowd, "When I am lifted up from the earth, I will draw all men to myself." Unless He was crucified, He could not save a single soul. He had to die so others could live.

The crowd was mystified. This didn't square with their view of God, the conqueror. They wanted earthly answers to eternal problems. Christ didn't promise them

An Easter Walk

that. In fact, He warned them that He would be with them only a little longer. They would have to decide if they were willing to lose all to serve Him.

During our Easter walk, we have to make the same decision. Are we willing to die to our wants so that we can live for Christ? May we chose to live for Him!

For a further walk, see
John 12:20-36   Related Passages
                        Matthew 10:39, 16:24-25
                        Mark 9:34-38
                        Luke 9:23-26

Day 7
I Believe, But...

I have come into the world as a light, so that no one who believes in me should stay in darkness. John 12:46

The week He gave His all for us; Jesus encountered an all too common attitude. How many miraculous signs had He performed during His ministry? How many questions had He completely answered during this week? What more proof did people need?

What was needed wasn't more proof, but the willingness to believe whole-heartedly. How many times have you heard someone say, "I believe you, but…" or have you said it yourself? Many of the Jewish leaders came to Him quietly this week and said exactly that. "We believe, but we fear the Pharisees who control the Temple." It is possible to sum up this attitude as "going along to get along." Moses had this attitude also. Even after the burning bush and the staff that became a snake, he still hesitated and made excuses.

An Easter Walk ✞✞✞

What are our excuses? Is it "I'm scared," or maybe it is "I'm not able." How about "I'm not smart enough" or, worst of all, "I'm already too busy with other jobs for You, God?" What keeps us from fully accepting His love, salvation, and the understanding that God is in control? What is our excuse? Do we believe He is who He has said and proved He is, or not?

May we, during our Easter walk, find ourselves on our knees accepting Him into all of our lives and not just stopping at "lip service"!

సౌర

For a further walk, see
John 12:37-50

Day 8
Lessons from the Pharisees

Woe to you, teachers of the law and Pharisees, you hypocrites! You give a tenth of your spices—mint, dill and cummin. But you have neglected the more important matters of the law—justice, mercy and faithfulness. You should have practiced the latter, without neglecting the former. Matthew 23:23

Have you ever heard the saying, "Practice what you preach?" I'm guessing it's often! Jesus said it to the Pharisees many times and at no time is it as clear as during Holy Week. Their self-righteousness and self-aggrandizements at the expense of others was an attitude that Our Lord condemned.

Jesus listed the offenses clearly. The attitude of caring more about what others think than what God thinks is at the heart of the matter. They were described as cups clean on the outside, but dirty within, whitewashed tombs full of rot and decay, and covered in flowing robes with long prayer tassels while they cheated widows. Specific examples of the attitude included the

An Easter Walk

tithing of minor types of spices while neglecting the major laws of justice, mercy, and faithfulness. Jesus reminded them that their ancestors had killed the prophets of old and that they, themselves, would torture and kill the new ones He would send.

Today, many make loud proclamations of their religious beliefs seeking the praise of man. How many times have we read these passages and said, "God, I thank you I am not like this other man?" May we look in the mirror during our Easter walk and see the truth. Each of us finds ourselves wanting man's praise at some time. May Christ convict us to clean the inside of our cup when we think this way!

For a further walk, see

Matthew 23	Related Passages
Mark 12:38-40	Matthew 6:1-8
Luke 20:45-47	Luke 18:9-14

Day 9
Keep on Working

Therefore keep watch, because you do not know the day or the hour. Matthew 25:13

Have you ever observed children's behavior when the parents or teachers are absent? They assume that freedom means it's time to play and goof off from their assignments. Have we outgrown this or do we slack up when our boss isn't looking? Be honest. Jesus understood fully the nature of us all and warned his disciples about how they should respond after His crucifixion and death. In three parables, our Lord makes it clear what He expects ... and how some will fall short of the mark.

The first parable features the Ten Virgins waiting for the Bridegroom's arrival. Five prepared with extra oil for their lamps and five did not. Those who ran out of oil found themselves left out of the banquet. We need to take heed and prepare to work for our Lord until He comes and not run out of desire or effort.

An Easter Walk

The second parable is about the talents handed out to three servants. The first two wisely invested and used their talents to generate more for their Master. The third servant simply sat idle and returned nothing to his master because of his lack of effort. Jesus reminds us that His talents and gifts are for us to use for His glory not for us to hoard.

The sheep and goats of the third parable were both taken by surprise by the Master's judgment. Those who understood His command to serve others found out that they were serving the Master as well. Those who chose to ignore service to others were surprised to find out that they had ignored their Master.

How to live our lives is underscored by these three parables. Jesus is clear that we are to be prepared to work for the long haul, to use the talents He has given us, and to serve others. May we honestly assess ourselves by these standards during our Easter walk. How can we improve even when we think the Master is not watching?

For a further walk, see
Matthew 25

Day 10
A Jar of Perfume or 30 Pieces of Silver

"Leave her alone," Jesus replied. "It was meant that she should save this perfume for the day of my burial." John 12:7

What a story of contrasts! Judas has grown weary waiting for Jesus to act. He seems to be tired out from wondering when hated Rome can be overthrown. If Jesus was the King, where were the riches for His followers? Then, one evening in Bethany, Judas saw an act of devotion of the most wasteful type. Mary broke an alabaster jar of nard and anointed Jesus with it. The nard was expensive—worth a year's wages—and used to prepare bodies for burial. The scripture accounts show Judas and other disciples to be critical of this waste. Why the money could have been spent to help the poor!

Jesus, seeing their hearts as always, rebuked them. He knew Mary's gift was a way to prepare Him for His coming burial, but more importantly, He knew her heart.

An Easter Walk

Mary didn't follow Him for her own gain, but because He was the one and only God, her Lord and Savior.

Our motives matter to Christ. Why *do* we go to church or give our tithes? Why *do* we read our Bibles or help others? Do we seek gain for ourselves because we will "look good." Are we willing to give our all to serve Him who gave so much more?

May we search our own hearts during our Easter walk and seek to give our all instead of seeking our self-centered goals.

For a further walk, see
Matthew 26:1-16
Mark 14:1-11
Luke 22:1-6
John 12:2-8

The Seed

How does a seed feel
Buried in the ground?
Shut off from air, light, sound?

Does it complain
About its life and loss,
Or quietly die to the old dross?

Does it try to hold life in,
Denying this path and cry,
Asking the Creator why?

Or does it remember that death to self
Causes one seed to grow
Creating more seeds for the Creator to sow?

An Easter Walk

Day 11
Unleavened Bread

"Say to the owner of the house he enters, 'The Teacher asks: Where is my guest room, where I may eat the Passover with my disciples?' He will show you a large upper room, furnished and ready. Make preparations for us there." Mark 14:14-15

Jesus sent two disciples to prepare for the Feast of Unleavened Bread during the Passover Celebration. As Exodus 12 explains, no yeast could be in the house nor used in the bread. Why was this provision made? It seems strange, doesn't it?

Think back to the First Passover. The Israelites had to be ready to leave Egypt when God said, "Go." If the cook had used yeast in that day's bread, she would be waiting on it to rise. They would not want to leave their bread and the hard work it took to make it. The temptation would be to wait on the bread, not the Lord.

What about us? What leavening do we allow into our lives? Is there something we are so attached to that we hesitate to leave it and what it represents when God says, "Go?" May we be ready during our Easter walk. Pray that God will lead us to recognize and remove the "leaven" from our lives.

ଛେଠ

For a further walk, see
Matthew 26:17-19
Mark 14:12-16
Luke 22:7-13

Related Passage
Exodus 12:14-20

An Easter Walk ✟✟✟

Day 12
The Lord's Supper

This is my blood of the covenant, which is poured out for many for the forgiveness of sins. Matthew 26:28

How many times have we heard "This do in remembrance of me?" Has the Lord's Supper become an empty ritual, or do we see it as a meaningful memorial to Christ's ultimate sacrifice for our salvation?

Paul warns us about participating in this sacrament in an unworthy manner in 1 Corinthians. What are some of the ways in which we can sully the significance? When we are thoughtless of why Christ instituted the memorial and go through the formality, we reduce it to empty ritual. When we are concentrating on other things we need to do, we reduce it to just another part of our agenda. When we are concentrating on what other people have done to us, we make a mockery of the sacrifice. Scripture gives us examples of each of these attitudes. The Corinthians had thoughtlessly made the Supper into an orgy in which some gorged and others did without. Judas had other "to do's" on his mind.

✝✝✝   *Steadham*

James and John were jealously watching the other disciples for signs of who would be first among them.

May we all examine our own motives and attitudes during our Easter walk. May we put all other thoughts aside and participate in the Lord's Supper as it was intended—as a meaningful memorial to Christ's sacrifice, the sacrifice that saves our souls.

೩೦೦೩

For a further walk, see
Matthew 26:26-29
Mark 14:22-25
Luke 22:17-20

Related Passage
1 Corinthians 11:23-29

An Easter Walk ✞✞✞

Day 13
The Servant

So He got up from the meal, took off His outer clothing, and wrapped a towel around His waist. After that, He poured water into a basin and began to wash His disciples' feet, drying them with the towel that was wrapped around Him. John 13:4-5

Pride and ambition are common among Christians today and the disciples were not immune either. Whether James and John or their mother asked about their position in the Kingdom of Heaven makes no difference—the attitude *was* prevalent among the disciples. Jesus *had* to root it out, if they were to be His messengers to the world.

Jesus used a common practice—the hospitality of washing guests' feet—to teach proper humility and service. All of the disciples would have bathed earlier in the day to be physically and ritually clean for the Passover meal, but their sandaled feet would be covered with dirt. A basin, pitcher, and towel were part of the provisions the two disciples had arranged earlier, but there was no servant to do the washing. At least that was what the disciples would think.

Jesus amazed them. As their Lord and Master, it would be unthinkable for Him to provide such a menial service. In fact, Peter protested loudly. None of the disciples had offered to render this service for the others though. All of them received a great lesson along with their clean feet—we are to serve others' needs, no matter how demeaning.

Do you hesitate at this command? Are there areas of service you cannot bring yourself to do? Why? Are you greater than Christ? Jesus made His personal example very clear and unmistakable. He said, "No servant is greater than his master, nor is the messenger greater than the one who sent him" and "I, your Lord and Teacher, have washed your feet, you also should wash one another's feet."

This coming Holy Week, may we learn to serve wholeheartedly—not self-servingly because we think we will be rewarded or grudgingly only because He commanded it. Gratitude should accompany our service, because He has washed not only our feet, but our hearts, souls, and spirits as well.

For a further walk, see
Luke 22:24-30
John 13:1-17

Related Passages
Matthew 20:20-28
Mark 10:35-45

An Easter Walk　　　　　　✝✝✝

Day 14
The Way

Jesus answered, "I am the way and the truth and the life. No one comes to the Father except through me." John 14:6

Do you ever get lost? Be honest! How do you feel—bewildered, scared? How do you handle it? Do you ask for directions? Do you keep going in circles until you see a landmark? The disciples were well aware of this feeling. After Jesus told them that they all would fall away, be scattered, and would deny Him, they felt lost and bewildered.

At this point, Jesus utters some words we have *all* depended on in times of crisis—"Do not be troubled." He explained the reason—that He would leave them to prepare a place for them, but He would return and they knew where He was going. Before we judge the disciples too harshly for being confused, we must admit that we also get lost while following Jesus.

Jesus patiently explained that He is "the Way, the Truth and the Light" and that all is revealed through our belief in Him. We can know God, see God, and find our way. Even when we are troubled and grieving, we can regain our footing and direction by remembering that Jesus shows us the way to joy. All we have to do is ask for God's help in Jesus' name. We have a choice. We can wander around lost and bewildered, following our own paths or ask Him to lead us.

May we all find His way during our Easter walk! Ask. He will calm our troubled hearts, show us God, and fill us with joy.

For a further walk, see
John 14:1-14
John 16:17-33

An Easter Walk

Day 15
"I am the True Vine"

I am the vine; you are the branches. If a man remains in me and I in him, he will bear much fruit; apart from Me you can do nothing. John 15:5

Have you ever pruned a bush or tree? What is the first thing you cut away? It's the branch that has quit flowering and bearing fruit, isn't it? What happens to the cut branch? It withers and dies. Then you prune old wood from producing branches to allow new fruit room to grow.

Jesus gave that image to us in this scripture. He vividly describes our job as branches of His vine—to bear fruit. If we don't, we are pruned of old wood or things that get in our way. The old, useless wood is burned. If we bear fruit, we will be pruned to produce more fruit.

His command to remain in Him and love each other explains how important bearing fruit is. In fact, we can't bear fruit unless we stay in the vine—in His will. We can do *nothing* without the vine—without Christ.

How often do we desire to bear fruit, but think we have "enough of Jesus" to do it on our own? Too often, isn't it? Jesus is clear—there can be no fruit unless we are in Him. Our desire should be to follow His commands and allow Him to produce fruit that lasts through us.

May we seek, this coming Holy Week, to remain in Jesus, the True Vine. By remaining in God's Plans on our Easter walk, we will grow luxuriantly and vigorously and will produce lasting fruit.

For a further walk, see
John 15:1-17

An Easter Walk ✞✞✞

Day 16
You Will Not Be Alone

And I will ask the Father, and He will give you another Counselor to be with you forever—the Spirit of Truth. John 14:16-17a

What could be more wonderful than living with Jesus day in and day out? Surely, that would keep us fully in the True Vine, wouldn't it? According to Jesus the answer is no. Surprised? The disciples were, but Jesus was very clear. They would have a much better life if He left them. It seems impossible, but God's plan is always better than what we can plan ourselves.

Jesus prepared the disciples for such a marvelous event that would take place after His death and resurrection. The Holy Spirit—God's third aspect—would come and live *inside* the disciples. The disciples could live in peace and love and not in fear only if the Spirit came. They would find God's own words coming from their mouths instead of physically having to ask Jesus what to say and do next.

✝✝✝ *Steadham*

Jesus knew that the disciples' task ahead could be accomplished only if they, themselves, became the home of God. If they became His temple, He could speak to men directly. How amazing that sullen, sinful, hateful man could house the one true God! May we, during our Easter walk, make a commitment to allow the Holy Spirit more and more room *within* our lives.

For a further walk, see
John 14:15-31
John 16:5-16

Related Passage
1 John 4:7-19

An Easter Walk ✝✝✝

Let Me Be Mary

Lord, let me be Mary
Sitting at your feet,
Forgetting the list of what must be done,
Listening and learning from Your only Son.

Lord, let me be Mary
Released from the demons of my mind,
Rising, following You,
Learning from my pain
And recognizing Your voice when
You call my name.

Lord, let me be Mary
Feeling You grow in my heart
As she felt You grow in her womb,
Both of us rejoicing that
You are not in the empty tomb.

Lord, let me be like each Mary,
Who knew You so well,
Having an intimate story to tell,
Realizing You can be as real to me today,
As to those who walked beside
You during the steps of Your earthly stay.

Day 17
Jesus Prayed

My prayer is not for them alone. I pray also for those who will believe in me through their message. John 17:20

On Thursday night, after establishing the Lord's Supper and promising the Holy Spirit would come, Jesus prayed. Both the intercessory prayer and the Gethsemane prayer show Jesus at His finest hour. Since the last step of His mission on Earth was at hand, He assessed what had been accomplished and what He had left to do.

As He thanked God for the harvest of His ministry, He prayed for the continuing mission. The disciples had learned of the Father and now, they were to continue to spread the Word. Jesus knew both the disciples and those they led to God would be tempted and tried. He prayed that all of us would be protected from Satan in our temptations.

As He continued into Gethsemane, Jesus fully saw what was before Him—pain, abandonment, and

An Easter Walk

torturous separation from God—and He responded with prayer. He considered the possibility of stopping the next step three times, but instead of allowing temptation to win, He prayed for God's will to be done each of those three times.

The disciples had not followed His lead. They gave into the temptation and slept. How many times do we give in when temptations knock on our doors? How can we resist? We must follow Jesus' words and example. We must pray, for without God, we cannot overcome temptation. The act of stopping and praying allows God's power to bolster us, as it did so for Jesus in His most difficult hour.

We must allow this example of Jesus to become a practice for us all. May we, during our Easter walk, commit ourselves to following His example.

For a further walk, see
Matthew 26:36-46
Mark 14:32-42
Luke 22:39-46
John 17:1-26, 18:1

Day 18
You Will Deny

"Simon, Simon, Satan has asked to sift you as wheat. But I have prayed for you, Simon, that your faith may not fail. And when you have turned back, strengthen your brothers." Luke 22:31-32

    Have you ever had a friend who was fun to hang out with until others were around? Then you were left out, and you were hurt. Put yourself in Jesus' place—He was on trial for His life and not only did His friends desert Him, but one of them denied openly that he knew Jesus. This was the same friend, who so boldly declared that he would follow Jesus even unto death. To top it all off, Jesus had even predicted that this would happen.
    Peter had been bold when Jesus told the disciples he would die and they would all "fall away" and that He would see them again in Galilee. Peter declared that even if he had to die, he would not fall away. Jesus told Peter the full truth. Peter would not only desert Him during the night, but he would also deny he knew Jesus. In fact, all the disciples declared their steadfastness. Jesus stressed a truth that all of us need to pay attention

An Easter Walk

to—we all fall away at times. Satan is always attempting to sift us like wheat to see if our commitment is true.

Just like Peter and the other disciples, we aren't always committed. Take heart, though, what else did Jesus say that night? He reminded us of two important facts. One, He will go before us and meet us again when we repent and recommit ourselves. Two, just like Peter, we will then be able to strengthen others. Can we truly help others with their problems if we have not experienced that same trial? We must always keep the last command of this night in mind. "Love one another. As I have loved you, so you must love one another. All men will know that you are My disciples if you love one another." No matter how rejected or embarrassed we are by others, we must love them as Christ loved us. During our Easter walk, may we show that love.

For a further walk, see

Prediction
Matthew 26:31-35
Mark 14:27-31
Luke 22:31-34
John 13:31-38

Denial
Matthew 26:69-75
Mark 14:54, 66-72
Luke 22:54-62
John 18:15-18, 25-27

Day 19
Arrested

Jesus replied, "Friend, do what you have come for"…"Do you think I cannot call on my Father, and He will at once put at my disposal more than twelve legions of angels? But how then would the Scriptures be fulfilled that say it must happen in this way?" Matthew 26:50a, 53-54

Does prayer help in adversity? After the agonizing prayers in Gethsemane, Jesus could calmly face His arrest. What an example for us to follow!

Judas led the armed crowd of chief priests, elders, and soldiers into the garden. They threatened Him with swords and clubs, yet He neither panicked nor begged. As Judas identified Him with a kiss and the respectful term, "Rabbi," He did not condemn nor accuse. When Peter rashly cut off the ear of Malchus, He stopped the confrontation with a healing touch. In fact, Jesus *could* have called twelve legions of angels, but He had already vanquished this temptation with prayer.

An Easter Walk   ✟✟✟

Jesus did remind the leaders that they could have arrested Him publicly each day during Holy Week while He taught in the Temple. Then, He drew on the strength of prayer and faith in God's powerful plan to remind us all that His sacrifice was planned from the beginning and fulfilled the prophesies of old.

May we remember His example during our Easter walk and find our solace in prayer. When storm clouds close us in, may we have faith that God will bolster us. May we find ourselves on our knees!

☙☪

For a further walk, see
Matthew 26:47-56
Mark 14:43-52
Luke 22:47-53
John 18:1-11

Day 20
Before the Sanhedrin

**They all asked, "Are you the Son of God?"
He replied, "You are right in saying I am." Luke 22:70-71**

In Proverbs 6:16-19 God explains what He hates. He hates prideful eyes, lying, and the shedding of innocent blood. A heart that devises evil and bears false witness is hateful to God. Someone who stirs up dissension is also hateful to Him. Every one of these hateful actions is on display during Jesus' "trial" before the Sanhedrin.

The prideful Pharisees asserted that they held the key to serving God. That pride led them into planning Jesus' death. They plotted to shed His blood and their schemes began to unfold—arrest, trial, and execution. On Thursday night, Jesus was brought to an illegal trial held at Annas' house. False witnesses were produced and their testimony conflicted with each other. Jesus refused to be drawn into the pointless accusation, but the leaders were relentless to achieve their foregone verdict.

An Easter Walk   ✝✝✝

When the High Priest asked Jesus if He were the Son of God, Jesus answered him saying, "I am." At that, the Sanhedrin concluded that Jesus was guilty of blasphemy. They could not decide any other way unless they admitted their pride and power was unfounded. Jesus was bound and blindfolded. Then He was struck. During this illegal trial, Peter stood and watched from the courtyard. He did nothing to help Jesus and denied he knew His Lord, as predicted.

During our Easter walk, may we find our place in this event. Are we holding onto preconceived ideas about who Jesus is? Do we testify falsely about Jesus through our words and actions? Are we merely observers, trying to stay out of trouble? Or are we willing to stand with Our Savior when times are hard? May we find the truth and allow it to free us to serve Him more.

ଛଜ

For a further walk, see
Matthew 26:57-68   Related Passages
Mark 14:53-65   Proverbs 6:16-19
Luke 22:54, 66-71   John 11:45-47
John 18:13-14, 19-24

Day 21
Trial before Pilate

Jesus said, "My kingdom is not of this world. If it were, my servants would fight to prevent my arrest by the Jews. But now my kingdom is from another place." John 18:36

After an illegal trial before the Sanhedrin, Jesus was taken to Pilate, the Roman governor. The Jewish leaders had condemned Jesus to death for blasphemy, but didn't have the authority to carry out the sentence—only Pilate could and he didn't care about blasphemy. Pilate's job was to produce peace and taxes for Caesar. In fact, his earlier actions had caused some uproar—demanding worship of Caesar and bringing Caesar's image onto the Temple Mount. The very same leaders who had opposed him then, now needed a favor.

How could the leaders get Pilate to do their bidding? They accused Jesus of the one charge Pilate would care about—treason against Rome. Accusations of claiming to be King of the Jews, stirring up rebellion, and advocating nonpayment of taxes were made. Jesus'

An Easter Walk

answer was simple, "Yes, I am King of the Jews, but My kingdom is not of this world. Everyone who is of the truth hears My voice."

Pilate did know some of the truth. He knew the charges were false. He knew Jesus was amazing in His calm response. There was no evidence of treason. Pilate pronounced Jesus innocent. Pilate even consulted Herod, the Jewish ruler of Galilee, who had been given power by Rome, and Herod came to the same conclusion as Pilate. He sent Jesus back to the governor.

"What is the truth?" Pilate asked. It is a question we all must answer about Jesus. Who is He? May we, during our Easter walk, seek this answer more fully for He *is* the King of Kings.

౽ಁಂ

For a further walk, see
Matthew 27:1-2, 11-14
Mark 15:1-5
Luke 23:1-12
John 18:28-38

Day 22
Crucify Him

But they shouted, "Take Him away! Crucify Him!" "Shall I crucify your king?" Pilate asked. "We have no king but Caesar," the chief priests answered. John 19:15

Pilate was puzzled. He knew the man before him was innocent, yet the leaders continued to insist that Jesus be executed. Pilate tried one more time to get them to relent. During Passover Week, Pilate had been granting the release of one prisoner. Maybe, he could talk them into releasing Jesus. But the more Pilate insisted Jesus was innocent, the more the leaders incited the crowd to ask for Barabbas.

What irony! Barabbas was *actually* guilty of treason and murder. Once more, the leaders claimed Jesus was guilty of both blasphemy and treason. Pilate questioned Jesus and reminded Him that the governor's authority included the death penalty. Jesus calmly told Pilate the truth again, "You have no authority over me unless God allows it."

An Easter Walk ✞✞✞

As the crowd screamed "Crucify Him," the leaders taunted Pilate. If He released Jesus, he would be no friend of Caesar's. Pilate became fearful. The Roman governor could not afford for this accusation to reach Caesar. In one last exasperated question, Pilate asked, "Shall I crucify your king?" The chief priests answered, "We have no king, but Caesar." They, in their desire to rid themselves of Jesus, committed the blasphemy they claimed to hate!

Pilate finally agreed to their plan and handed Jesus over to the guard to be executed. May our Easter walk remind us that we, too, are guilty. May it not find us condemning others when we have also fallen short of God's standards. May we admit the truth—Jesus is King and He was crucified for us.

8003

For a further walk, see
Matthew 27:15-26
Mark 15:6-15
Luke 23:13-25
John 18:39-40, 19:1-16

Steadham

Thief

I scream.
>Fire in my hands and on my feet.
>My arms stretch.
>My shoulders part and tear.
>Each breath a struggle.
>My heart races toward explosion.
>Panic slams me.
>"Save yourself!" the crowds yell.
>I jerk out of my self-centered torment.
>Light glints off the helms, breastplates
>And spears of the soldiers.
>The taunts are not for me,
>But for the man in the middle.
>Some pray for Him and weep.
>But the other thief takes up the taunt.
>"You claim to be God! Save us!
>"You can't. You're a joke. Pathetic!"

I cry.
>"He isn't like us. Can't you see?
>Don't you fear God?
>He has done nothing wrong!"
>Turning to the man in the middle,
>I see love streaming from his pained face.
>"Jesus, remember me when
>You come into Your kingdom."
>His eyes lock into mine
>And peace stills my wild thoughts.
>He makes a promise,
>"I tell you the truth,
>Today you will be with me in Paradise."

I smile.

An Easter Walk ✟✟✟

Day 23
Mocking Jesus

They stripped Him and put a scarlet robe on Him, and then wove a crown of thorns and set it on His head. They put a staff in His right hand and knelt in front of Him and mocked Him. "Hail, King of the Jews!" they said. They spit on Him, and took the staff and struck Him on the head again and again. Matthew 27:28-30

Have you ever been mocked, treated with ridicule and contempt, and mimicked in derision? Most of us have been. How did you respond? We usually strike out with angry words filling our mouths or withdraw to nurse the wounds. Either way, we *do not* respond calmly and accept it. Our hearts seethe with shame and anger.

Every indignity the soldiers could imagine was heaped on Jesus. If He was a king, they thought, we'll mock how a king should be treated. Herod's soldiers dressed Him in a gorgeous robe of purple, the color of royalty. Pilate's soldiers placed a crown of thorns on His head. They placed a reed in His right hand as a scepter and bowed in mocking respect to Him as "King of the Jews." Then they beat Him about the head, having already scourged and whipped Him. Yet Jesus did not scream out. He did not curse them. He calmly accepted the soldiers' mistreatment. Pilate was amazed, and his amazement may have fueled his belief in Jesus' innocence. Yet, Pilate knew the political reality of the situation—this man must die. It was the only way to calm the Jewish leaders.

May we be amazed at our Savior's calm during our Easter walk. Amazed at the assurance He had that what He had to do was right. The only way to save us was to suffer more ridicule than any of us can imagine.

For a further walk, see
Matthew 27:27-32
Mark 15:16-20
Luke 23:6-12
John 19:1-3

An Easter Walk ✞✞✞

Day 24
To Golgotha and the Cross

The people stood watching, and the rulers even sneered at Him. They said, "He saved others; let Him save Himself if He is the Christ of God, the Chosen One." Luke 23:35

After a series of rushed trials with predetermined verdicts, after being whipped and beaten, Jesus was made to carry His cross to Golgotha. Is it any wonder that He stumbled under the load? Simon of Cyrene was pressed into service, and he carried the Cross the rest of the way.

What followed was a Roman execution for "crimes" against the Jewish leaders. Jesus was offered wine mixed with myrrh to deaden His wits to the pain. He refused. Why? How often do we seek to numb the pain when times are hard? Yet, Jesus chose to be fully aware of the pain of His sacrifice. Roman crucifixion killed the condemned slowly and painfully. The victim was required to hold himself up by the wounds in his feet and hands in order to breathe. Psalm 22 describes how it felt. Yet, Jesus chose to feel every bit of this pain.

While He suffered, the soldiers mocked Him. If He were God, if He could rebuild the Temple in three days, why didn't He save Himself? The leaders mocked Him the same way. Pilate, the judge, who wanted to know what was the truth, stated it plainly on the sign above His head—"Jesus of Nazareth, The King of the Jews." It infuriated the leaders, but Pilate refused to remove the sign. Without Pilate, the leaders could not execute Jesus, so they had to accept Pilate's decision.

This was the sacrifice which Jesus had come to make. This terrible pain saves us from judgment for our sins. It is this amazing Man who suffered this pain; who loved us more than His own life. During our Easter walk, may we seek to appreciate Jesus' life and death for our sins.

ഝര

For a further walk, see
Matthew 27:31-44
Mark 15:20-32
Luke 23:26-38
John 19:16-24

Related Passages
Psalm 22:14-18
Isaiah 53:5-9

An Easter Walk ✝✝✝

Day 25
What the Thief Learned

Jesus answered him, "I tell you the truth, today you will be with me in paradise." Luke 23:43

Our God is a God of justice and mercy. How can God demand both punishment for sin *and* give the grace of forgiveness if He is the same? That is a good question.

Justice demands payment. If you do the crime, be prepared to do the time as the thieves who shared Golgotha with Christ were doing. Our history and culture understands this very well, but we say—"if I can get away with it without getting caught..." It's a gamble we all love to take. The problem is God *always* catches us. We never get away with it. He made the laws and He has the evidence so we *will* be punished.

Then there is that other character trait of God—mercy. He loved us so much, He also provided us with a chance for redemption. He, Himself—almighty and just—came to live with us. He, Himself—perfect and blameless—paid the price for our sins and crimes. He,

Himself—all powerful and loving—allowed Himself to be beaten, cursed, and executed to give us mercy.

We have a choice. We can chose to take the gamble like one of the thieves on Good Friday. He rejected the offer, crying, "If You are the Christ, save Yourself and us." But the other thief recognizing his own guilt, said, "We are being punished justly." He asked the Lord of Mercy only to remember him. Immediately, God, the Merciful, accepted the man's honesty and took the punishment for him.

There is no contradiction here. There is only one all-loving God and He wants us to give Him a chance to redeem us. Justice and Mercy—what an amazing God! May we accept that mercy this coming Holy Week.

For a further walk, see
Luke 23:39-43

An Easter Walk

Day 26
Darkness During the Day

From the sixth hour until the ninth hour darkness came over all the land...At that moment the curtain of the temple was torn in two from top to bottom. The earth shook and the rocks split. Matthew 27:45, 51

How many people were going about their lives as usual that Friday? How many did not realize that God, Himself, was giving His life for them? How many needed His grace and mercy? The last question is easy to answer—*all* of them!

As the Creator of all nature voluntarily gave up His life, nature itself could not ignore what was happening and could not be silent. All of created glory mourned with three hours of darkness during the day and an earthquake. Such a sacrifice! Such a sorrow! How often do we go about our lives oblivious to what is happening around us? Do we realize the needs of others or think only of our own wants? Yet, nature was aware of the crucifixion of Christ.

When we take Christ's sacrifice for granted, we reject the truth even nature recognized. Can we sit idle during our Easter walk? May we always be aware of our surroundings and the others nearby. May we always be aware of our Lord's great and enduring love that sought to save us even as we were unaware that His sacrifice was necessary to save us.

For a further walk, see
Matthew 27:45-51
Mark 15:33-37
Luke 23:44-46

An Easter Walk ✞✞✞

Day 27
Jesus said...

And when the centurion, who stood there in front of Jesus, heard His cry and saw how He died, he said, "Surely this man was the Son of God!" Mark 15:39

    Darkness and the immense torment of carrying the sin of the world accompanied Jesus' last three hours on the cross. Since sin is a separation from God, Jesus felt the utter hopelessness of ultimate separation from the source of love, life, and goodness. His anguished cry of "My God, My God, why have You forsaken me!" tears at our hearts. It was for us that He had to feel this pain.

    As His sacrifice neared its close, He said, "I am thirsty." Sour wine mixed with water, probably from a soldier's rations, was offered and He drank. He knew His death was near and He gave Himself to God, the Father—"Father, into Your hands I commend my spirit." At last, a shout of victory came from our Lord when He cried, "It is finished!" Jesus then died.

    In their rush to have this execution completed before sundown and the Sabbath, the leaders asked that the three crucified men's legs be broken. That way they would only be able to hold themselves up with their wounded hands and death would come more rapidly. As the soldiers went about this grim task, they found Christ already dead. To insure their discovery, they speared Jesus' side and the rush of both blood and water confirmed their diagnosis.

In the wake of these events, the truth convicted at least one soldier, the Centurion. "Surely, this is the Son of God," was his fervent testimony. May we with the same conviction and desire, say, "Surely, He is God!" during our Easter walk.

❧☙

For a further walk, see
Matthew 27:45-54
Mark 15:33-39
Luke 23:44-47
John 19:25-37

An Easter Walk

Day 28
The Torn Veil

And the curtain of the temple was torn in two. Jesus called out with a loud voice, "Father, into your hands I commit my spirit." When He had said this, He breathed His last. Luke 23:45b-46

When the Tabernacle and Temple were built, there was one place into which only the High Priest could go—the Holy of Holies. As God's Spirit filled it, sinful man could not enter. Thick tapestries or veils hid it from man. Once a year, the High Priest sacrificed for his own sins and those of the congregation so that he could enter the Holy of Holies. However, on this Good Friday, the ritual ceased to be necessary.

Jesus died, as the final sacrifice for all our sins, and the veil tore from top to bottom. The Holy of Holies opened for all to enter in. Jesus, the perfect High Priest, sacrificed Himself for us and allowed each of us to enter into the presence of God. His ascension into Heaven allowed His Spirit to come and dwell within us. We became the temple of the Living God! Our bodies are His temple.

May we, during our Easter walk, accept this amazing offer and live for Him in a manner worthy of this great honor. May we realize that His great love allows us to personally approach God Almighty.

For a further walk, see
Matthew 27:51-53
Mark 15:38
Luke 23:45

Related Passage
1 Corinthians 6:19

An Easter Walk

It Is Finished!

It is finished—
> The promise of the Nativity
> Completed by Calvary.

It is finished—
> Our separation from God
> Ended by His love.

It is finished—
> The plan from the beginning
> Fulfilled at the end.

It is finished—
> The condemnation of sin
> Pardoned at the Cross.

It is finished—
> What was seen as failure
> Is victory made complete.

It is finished—
> God with us
> Living in our hearts.

Day 29
Jesus Was Buried

Later, Joseph of Arimathea asked Pilate for the body of Jesus. Now Joseph was a disciple of Jesus, but secretly because he feared the Jews. With Pilate's permission, he came and took the body. He was accompanied by Nicodemus, the man who earlier had visited Jesus at night. Nicodemus brought a mixture of myrrh and aloes, about seventy-five pounds. John 19:38-39

Sometimes, the need to put one foot in front of the other seems insurmountable. In the wake of a loved-one's death, we find ourselves shattered by grief, terrified by the loneliness, and yet we have to take care of the necessary arrangements for burial. Can we imagine all this pain intensified by the realization that the deceased is our Lord and Savior? That's where the disciples found themselves on the afternoon of Good Friday. Lost, alone, and fearful, some of them left Golgotha. Others, however, sought to honor their Lord.

An Easter Walk   ✟✟✟

Among those who stayed were Mary Magdalene, Mary the mother of James and Joseph, and Salome, Zebedee's wife and mother of James and John. Joseph of Arimathea went to Pilate and asked for the body of Jesus. Pilate, though surprised Jesus was already dead, granted the request. Joseph and Nicodemus, who brought the required spices for burial, then prepared the body and wrapped it in linen. The body was placed in a new tomb that Joseph had carved out of rock for his family. After the burial, Joseph had a stone rolled in front of the entrance.

It is so normal to us to see this care, but the cost was high. Both Joseph and Nicodemus were members of the Sanhedrin. By going into Pilate's house and by handling the dead body, the two men made themselves ritually unclean. They could not participate in Sabbath services the next day. They openly declared their respect and allegiance to Jesus by their actions. Nicodemus, who had come to Jesus by night to ask about His teachings, now was ready to show his love openly. Mary Magdalene and Mary, the mother of James and Joseph, watched over the preparations of the body. They planned to continue the care after the Sabbath.

Can we put ourselves in the sandals of these disciples? Can we feel the despair? May we, during our Easter walk, remember all who grieve and seek ways to help no matter what the personal cost.

༄༅

For a further walk, see

Matthew 27:55-61
Mark 15:40-47
Luke 23:48-55
John 19:38-42

An Easter Walk ✞✞✞

Day 30
Watching and Waiting

Then they went home and prepared spices and perfumes. But they rested on the Sabbath in obedience to the commandment. Luke 23:56

None of us likes to wait. We chafe when our food is slow in coming at a restaurant or our family doesn't get ready on time. There are worse times of waiting like when a child is very sick or a family member is slowly dying. We watch the clock creep slowly by outside the operating room or during the time between the death of a loved one and the funeral. Can we imagine anything worse than that?

The women who followed Jesus knew our feelings on the Saturday after Jesus died. They left the tomb before sunset Friday and prepared spices and perfumes for His body, but they could not continue their work until Sunday. How long did that Sabbath take to run its course? How weary did they grow while waiting?

Ironically, the Pharisees were very busy on that day of rest. They remembered Jesus' claim to rise again in three days, and made their way to Pilate yet again. This time, as they visited Pilate, they requested a guard for the tomb. Pilate agreed. His orders were simple—they were to seal the tomb and wait by it. Surely the Pharisees' fears of the disciples stealing the body had been prevented. They could rest.

What lesson can we draw from this Saturday of waiting? Can we learn to wait on the Lord's timing with patience? Can we stop our frenzied attempts to create the outcome we want? During our Easter walk, may we approach the Lord with patience—to wait on His will, plan, and timing for our lives.

For a further walk, see
Matthew 27:62-66
Luke 23:56

An Easter Walk ✝✝✝

Day 31
The Women at the Tomb

Then Jesus said to them, "Do not be afraid. Go and tell my brothers to go to Galilee; there they will see me." Matthew 28:10

We don't know if it was it cloudy and overcast that first Easter Sunday morning, but we can understand how Mary Magdalene, Mary, and Salome felt. They had followed Jesus from Galilee, to the cross, and to the tomb. They could only think of one other service they could do for their Lord. Therefore, they bought and prepared the necessary spices to anoint His body and went to the tomb. Along the way, they wondered how they would move the massive stone so they could follow through with their plan. Can we imagine how much heavier than the stone their hearts were?

Then, as they came to the tomb, they made an amazing discovery. The stone had been rolled away! Cautiously, they went into the tomb to do their duty, but did not find a body. Two angels greeted them with wonderful news—Jesus wasn't dead! He had been resurrected and the women were reminded that this would happen. A new command was given—to go tell the good news to the believers. As they ran back, Jesus surprised the women. He appeared and He reminded them not to be afraid. He would be with all His believers. They should share their good news.

What stone sits in our paths? Do we see nothing, but gloom and burden? During our Easter walk, may we remember Jesus will always be with us. He will always help us with our burdens. May we seek Him no matter how heavy our load.

For a further walk, see
Matthew 28:1-10
Mark 16:2-8
Luke 24:1-8

Day 32
Mary Magdalene

Jesus said to her, "Mary."
She turned toward Him and cried out in Aramaic, "Rabboni!" (which means Teacher)...
Jesus said ... "Go instead to my brothers and tell them, 'I am returning to my Father and your Father, to my God and your God.'" John 20:16, 17b

Who was Mary Magdalene? There have been many speculations over time. Some have equated her with the prostitute who was about to be stoned. Recently, some have said she was Jesus' wife. Scripture doesn't support either portrayal. Mary is described as a woman possessed by demons. Jesus had freed her from that torture. She had shown her gratitude by becoming one of His followers. Mary was at the cross and she watched the burial. On Easter Sunday, she was ready to continue her service. Planning with the other women to use the spices and perfumes on His body, she found that her plans were unnecessary.

Steadham

When the women found the stone rolled away and the body gone, Mary ran back to get Peter and John. After they left the garden, Mary remained. She looked into the tomb and the angels asked her why she wept. She asked, "Where have they taken My Lord's body?" As she turned back to the garden, she saw Jesus, but grief still clouded her eyes. She asked her question again, but the answer wasn't what she expected.

When Jesus said her name, Mary recognized Him. Can we even imagine the joy of this loyal, devoted follower? Can we see her desire to be with the one she thought was dead? To her surprise, Jesus gave her a mission. Go and tell the others that you have seen the Lord. The fact is we can all know exactly how Mary felt. Each of us can come to know Jesus just as well as she did. He can call our names just as clearly. More important, is the fact that we, too, have the mission to go and tell.

May we remember, during our Easter walk, to seek Jesus. May we remember that the tomb is empty and we have a mission to tell others that we have seen the Lord.

For a further walk, see
Mark 16:9-11
John 20:1-2, 11-18

Related Passages
Luke 8:1-3
Matthew 27:56

An Easter Walk ✝✝✝

Day 33
Peter

Again Jesus said, "Simon son of John, do you truly love me?"
He answered, "Yes, Lord, you know that I love you."
Jesus said, "Take care of my sheep." John 21:16

Peter was the most colorful of the apostles—always speaking when questions were asked. He showed great faith, whether answering Christ's question, "Who do you say I am?" or climbing out of the boat for a walk on the waves. His assertive nature also led to rash mistakes, whether he was "instructing" Jesus that He would not die or cutting off the ear of the high priest's servant in Gethsemane. How depressed was Peter that Saturday after the crucifixion? How often did he feel anger at himself for denying Christ? How hopeless did his life seem at this time?

When the women came to him Easter Sunday with an amazing account of the empty tomb, Peter again acted quickly. He ran to see for himself. Once he arrived, Peter found the stone rolled away and saw only an empty grave with clothes in place of Christ's body. What thoughts chased his sorrow? We don't know, but we do know he wondered what had happened. We do know Christ appeared to Peter along with the others that night in the upper room. We know Peter was restored to Christ's fellowship.

Along the shores of the Sea of Galilee, Christ sought Peter out for a private conversation. The Lord asked Peter, "Do you love me?" three times. Three times, Peter answered yes. Three times, Christ gave Peter the command to care for Christ's followers. Three times, Peter accepted the command and replaced the three denials with service. When earthly concerns caught Peter's attention again, Christ reminded him, "Follow me." Peter obeyed.

Peter grew into a leader of the church. No matter how hard his lessons had been, Peter showed what faith could do. During our Easter walk, may we follow Peter's example and be ready to confess our belief in Christ. May we be ready to care for others and ready to follow Christ wherever He wants us to go.

For a further walk, see

Luke 24:12
John 20:3-10
John 21:15-22

Related Passages
Matthew 14:22-36, 16:13-28
Mark 8:27-38
Luke 9:18-27

An Easter Walk

Day 34
John

Finally the other disciple, who had reached the tomb first, also went inside. He saw and believed. John 20:8

What character trait do we often use when describing the apostle John? It is love. In fact, some have counted how many times he wrote about Christian love. It is mentioned more than twenty-five times in his three short letters. Yet, a loving-nature was not his main character trait when he met Christ.

John and his brother, James, were nicknamed "sons of thunder" by Christ due to their hot-tempered natures. This trait shows up at other times as jealousy and ambition. When John saw others who weren't among the twelve working miracles in Jesus' name, he wanted Christ to rebuke them. He asked to be placed at Jesus' right hand when He came into the Kingdom of Heaven. None of these actions stem from a loving nature.

Daily learning from Christ worked an amazing change in John. He followed Jesus to the trials on Thursday night and was present at the Cross. Jesus asked John to care for His mother, Mary, after His death. When the news of the empty tomb came, John ran to the garden and then hesitated. The impetuous, young man had changed. John finally went into the tomb, and believed the women's story, but freely admitted that he did not yet fully understand its meaning.

After seeing Christ that night in the upper room and walking with Him until the Ascension, John was fully transformed. Christ's love made John the apostle who taught Christ's greatest commandment—to love one another. May we, during our Easter walk, be as filled with Christ's love as John was. May we remember that it is through our love that we prove we are followers of Christ. It is by our love that we obey Him best.

For a further walk, see
John 20:3-10, 19-23

Related Passages
Mark 3:17, 9:38
Mark 10:35-37
1 John 2:9-11
1 John 3:10-18
1 John 4:7-12

An Easter Walk

The Valley Walk

Down the path I went,
Head dropped, all energy spent.
Tears obscure my sight.
I see nothing; all is night.

Water runs from the mountaintop
And it is, here, in the low place I stop.
Cruelly, I see where I want to be—
At the top of the mountain, in glory.

Dirt piles into the ditches and dips.
Into depression and despair I slip.
How can I lift my head and raise my eye
Where only desert and desolation lie?

Then the dreary clouds of pain
Gradually clear and leave again.
Light, at first weak and wan,
Grows to a stronger and stronger dawn.

It is then in the ditches full of dirt
I see more than just pain and hurt.
Someone has planted a lily to grow
And the touch of the Creator can show.

Only where the water leaves rich soil
Can life and its beauty be able to toil,
Thriving and flourishing as the Creator planned,
To grow as He places it in His hand.

Steadham

And so it is on the path of the valley walk
That my God, the Creator, and I can talk.
And with the lily I can grow,
His glory and goodness to show.

Here the Creator meant me to be,
To grow and bloom for others to see.
As I accept the care of His loving hand,
They see my beauty as He planned.

An Easter Walk　✝✝✝

Day 35
Road to Emmaus

When He was at the table with them, He took bread, gave thanks, broke it and began to give it to them. Then their eyes were opened and they recognized Him, and He disappeared from their sight. Luke 24:30-31

How often do we move through life unaware of our surroundings? How often do cares and concerns distract us? That's the situation in which Cleopas and his companion found themselves on Easter Sunday. As they walked toward Emmaus, they discussed the terrible events of Holy Week. They knew the tomb had been found empty, but they had not heard that Jesus had been seen. Deep despair had settled over these two disciples. All their hopes and dreams seemed shattered on the cross at Golgotha.

A stranger joined them and asked about the conversation. They shared their burden and got a gift in return. Jesus, who they did not recognize, explained God's entire plan, including the scriptures that predicted

✟✟✟   *Steadham*

the Messiah's sacrifice. As day turned to dusk, the disciples invited Jesus to stay with them and eat supper. Jesus broke the bread and blessed it, and their eyes were opened. The Messiah lived! Jesus disappeared and left them with the Good News. Immediately, even though it was now night, Cleopas and his friend hurriedly returned to Jerusalem. They *had* to share this news with the others. The rest had gathered in the upper room and listened to the story, but doubt still filled them. Their grief was so distracting.

During our Easter walk, may we find ourselves willing to put aside our distractions and worries. May we be receptive to the Good News—The Messiah lives!

For a further walk, see
Mark 16:12-13
Luke 24:13-35

An Easter Walk

Day 36
The Priests' Reaction

When the chief priests had met with the elders and devised a plan, they gave the soldiers a large sum of money, telling them, "You are to say, 'His disciples came during the night and stole Him away while we were asleep.'" Matthew 28:12-13

The disciples had been filled with wonder and doubt as more and more of their group reported seeing Jesus this day, but there was another group that found the news anything but wonderful. As the women went to tell the disciples, some of the guards who had experienced the earthquake and watched the stone roll away, went to the chief priests. Their story was met with intense anger and great fear.

The priests' worst nightmare had been the disciples stealing Christ's body, but the truth had to be even more devastating. Not only was the body gone, but there wasn't any proof that the disciples had stolen it either. What could the leaders do? They chose the same dishonest path they had used during Jesus' trial—they paid for false witnesses. The Roman soldiers were paid to testify that the disciples had, indeed, stolen Christ's body. They were also assured that if the story found its way to Pilate, the leaders would defend the soldiers. What a web of deceit!

We can only wonder at how hard the priests and elders fought to retain power and control. They refused to believe Jesus for fear of losing their positions. We also have to admit that we fight just as hard sometimes when we fear God's will. We also want to stay in control of our lives. May we, during our Easter walk, surrender all that we cling to; all we fear losing. May we find peace in Christ's love.

For a further walk, see
Matthew 28:11-15

An Easter Walk   ✞✞✞

Day 37
The Upper Room

Again Jesus said, "Peace be with you! As the Father has sent me, I am sending you." John 20:21

That Easter Sunday must have been an emotional roller coaster for the disciples! They woke in heavy despair and deep grief for their Lord was dead. Then some felt surprise at the empty tomb. Fear of the leaders and their manufactured witnesses shadowed any small hope that had begun to flicker. The others doubted the disciples who had seen Christ. After this emotional day, they gathered in the upper room, the recent site of their last meal with Jesus. The discussion had to be intense.

As the discussion proceeded, a miracle occurred—Jesus was with them! Can we imagine the startling sight? How many hearts began to hammer? What were they seeing? Christ, as always, knew their hearts and said the very things they needed to hear. "Peace be with you" and "Why are you troubled?" were His words. As amazement gave way to joy, he showed them His hands and side. He ate with them, and then He opened their minds to understanding. All of the scriptures had led to this event—Moses, the prophets, and Psalms. Christ reminded them of their mission. "I am sending you as my Father sent me." Again, they were promised the Holy Spirit as their guide and comforter.

Can we imagine the joy and gratitude the disciples felt? In truth, we don't have to imagine—we can feel it for ourselves. During our Easter walk, may we be in Christ's presence, feeling at peace, full of understanding, and ready to continue His mission.

For a further walk, see
Mark 16:14
Luke 24:36-44
John 20:19-23

Day 38
Thomas

Then Jesus told him, "Because you have seen me, you have believed; blessed are those who have not seen and yet have believed." John 20:29

On Easter Sunday, Thomas had been absent from the upper room. He had missed Jesus' appearance. As the others insisted they had seen Jesus, Thomas refused to believe. He *had* seen Jesus crucified, so how could He be alive? In fact, Thomas had specific criteria for believing—he would *have* to see the nail marks in Jesus' hands and put his own hand into the spear wound in Jesus' side.

One week later, Thomas was in the upper room with the others. The doors were locked and yet, Jesus still appeared. His words were calming, "Peace be with you." Then He turned to His doubting disciple and offered the proof Thomas had demanded. Suddenly, Thomas found the physical proof unnecessary and cried, "My Lord and my God!" Jesus blessed those who would believe without physically seeing Him.

Before we react with disapproval of Thomas or with smug self-congratulation that we have believed without seeing, we need to ask ourselves, "What do we not believe about Jesus?" Do we always believe that He forgives us, or do we cling to a sin in order to punish ourselves? Do we always believe that he will take care of us or do we wonder if that's still true as a new trial unfolds? Do we always believe that He loves us, or do we believe Satan's lies that we are unlovable? Do we always believe that He is with us, or do we feel alone in our despair? During our Easter walk, may we believe all that He has told us. May we believe that He saves, forgives, and loves us, and that He will be with us always and forever.

For a further walk, see
John 20:24-31

An Easter Walk ✞✞✞

Day 39
At the Sea of Galilee

He said, "Throw your net on the right side of the boat and you will find some." When they did, they were unable to haul the net in because of the large number of fish. John 21:6

The Lord sometimes answers our prayers with the command to wait. We don't usually like that answer. In fact, we usually chafe and whine when we realize that is what God wants us to do. We can only wonder how the disciples felt as they followed Christ's command to return to Galilee and wait for Him. We do know that they followed His command. Seven of them decided to go fishing on the Sea of Galilee while they waited. It was a good choice since it was the previous occupation of Peter, James, John, and Andrew.

After fishing all night, though, they had caught no fish and were ready to return to shore when someone called out to them asking if they had any fish. It was Jesus, but they didn't recognize Him. Jesus then told them to cast their nets on the right side of the boat.

Suddenly, their nets were so full they could not even haul them on board. John recognized who had spoken to them and Peter swam ashore to see Jesus. As Jesus prepared breakfast for them, He told them to bring in their catch. Even though there were 153 fish in the nets, they did not break. None of the disciples questioned who Jesus was. None of them questioned the amazing provision of the catch. They had grown since some of them had met Jesus while fishing three years before. They had learned that He always provided what was needed and provided it in abundance.

What about us? Do we accept the answer to wait from God? Do we always remember that His plan will provide with amazing abundance of what we need? May we, during our Easter walk, wait patiently on the Lord. Just think how many fish we will catch if we do!

ଛଡ଼

For a further walk, see
John 21:1-14

An Easter Walk ✟✟✟

Day 40
The Ascension and Commission

But you will receive power when the Holy Spirit comes on you; and you will be my witnesses in Jerusalem, and in all Judea and Samaria, and to the ends of the earth. Acts 1:8

As they traveled to Bethany and the Mount of Olives, the disciples' excitement must have increased. There were more than five hundred this time and this visit with the Living Lord had been arranged beforehand. All the other meetings had been surprises and Jesus had said, "Peace be with you" to calm their fears and startled thoughts. This time, though, they knew it would be different and special. How many still clung to the belief that an earthly kingdom was approaching rapidly? We don't know, but we do know the real reason for the meeting was even more miraculous.

When Jesus appeared to them, the disciples worshipped Him, and He explained their mission one more time. They would preach the Good News—Jesus saves—starting in Jerusalem and Judea and they would spread the message to the whole world. How many questioned their ability to do this? We don't know, but we do know they were assured that it would not depend on them alone. Jesus commanded that they return to Jerusalem until God's promised gift of the Holy Spirit came to them. Through God's power, they would be able to complete the mission.

Then Jesus ascended into Heaven. Many among them were dismayed. How on earth, were they going to carry out this plan? What had happened to their dreams of an earthly kingdom? Jesus didn't leave them without reassurance. Two angels reminded them that Jesus would return.

While on our Easter walk, may we remember that we, too, are a part of this mission. We, too, are not required to carry it out by ourselves. We, too, can have the Holy Spirit of God and we, too, can help save the world.

For a further walk, see
Matthew 28:16-20
Mark 16:15-20
Luke 24:44-53
Acts 1:3-12

Related Passages
1 Corinthians 15:6

An Easter Walk

During Your Easter Walk

Have you experienced the Living Lord?
    Seen the Cross?
    Been to the tomb?
    Felt His scars?
    Seen the storm pass?
    Felt the earth tremble?
    Been filled with joy?
    Felt faith take flight?
    Your soul filled with calm assurance?

During your Easter walk,
May you come to the Cross
And see for yourself—
He lives!

Acknowledgments

No writer creates a book in isolation. All of them have people to thank and I am no different. I could not have written *An Easter Walk* without the support and encouragement from many of the people in my life. I want to thank them for answering questions, holding my hand when I got discouraged and thinking of many of the things I needed to do, but had forgotten.

- Martha and Thea Stallings, my mother and sister, for encouragement and close reading of the first version of this book
- Susan Edwards, my dear friend, for upper notes when I got discouraged and close reading
- Mary Wilburn, my dear friend and fellow writer, for not letting me give up on finishing and printing *An Easter Walk*
- Mary Cunningham and Diana Black for answering my interminable questions about how to create the cover
- Susan Mashburn, pastor's secretary of First Baptist Church, for setting up and copying the first version that was used by the congregation during Lent 2007

An Easter Walk

- ❖ The members of the Carrollton Creative Writers Club for all their encouragement
- ❖ The congregation of First Baptist Church Carrollton for reading and studying the first version and encouraging me to print it for others to use
- ❖ Steve Davis, pastor of First Baptist Church Carrollton, for the challenge to truly prepare to worship during Lent that started this study
- ❖ My husband, John, for everything—it's impossible to list it all
- ❖ And most important, the Lord God, my Creator, Savior, and Sustainer, for inspiration, love, and life

May this Easter and all the rest you celebrate be a joyous walk in the light of His love.

Zan Marie Steadham
Ad Gloriam Dei
To the Glory of God

✝✝✝ *Steadham*